Horse care with
Caddie

Carola von Kessel

Illustrations by
Irmtraud Guhe

Contents

- Welcome to Caddie's Equine Academy! ... 3
- *Horsey know-how: How much looking after do horses need?* ... 4
- *How to: Before grooming* ... 8
- *Fun & Games: How to look after your horse* ... 10
- *How to: Hoofcare step by step* ... 12
- *How to: Grooming step by step* ... 15
- *Fun & Games: Seasonal change* ... 22
- *How to: Finishing touches* ... 24
- *Fun & Games: How do horses groom themselves?* ... 28
- Solution ... 30
- Index ... 32

Imprint

Copyright © 2003 by
Cadmos Verlag GmbH, Brunsbek
Gestaltung + Satz: Ravenstein, Verden
Illustrationen: Irmtraud Guhe
Druck: Westermann Druck, Zwickau

Alle Rechte vorbehalten. Abdrucke oder Speicherung in elektronischen Medien nur nach vorheriger schriftlicher Genehmigung durch den Verlag.

Printed in Germany

ISBN 3-86127-049-5

NORTH LINCOLNSHIRE LIBRARIES	
3003389556	
Peters Books	05-Apr-05
Gox 3/06	£6.95

Caddie & Jacky

Welcome to Caddie's Equine Academy!

Hello, my name is Caddie – and I'm a rather special pony. Together with my young owner Jacky, I'd like to show all my young friends how they should act around horses and how to look after them properly.

We've also come up with some fun puzzles for you to test how much you've learnt about horse care.

Horse care is not just about grooming or picking out your horse's hooves. When you groom your horse it can help to form a special bond between you both and that's what you want, isn't it?

So, have fun reading this book and grooming your horse!

Best wishes

Caddie

Horsey know-how

How much looking after do horses need?

Horse care in the wild

• Most horses enjoy rolling — especially when they've been sweating and their skin itches.

Why do horses need grooming? Simple: in the wild, wind, rain, sun and snow all help to look after a horse's skin and coat.
The wind blows away any dead skin cells and rain moistens the skin. If the skin of a horse living outdoors itches anywhere, he will scratch himself on a tree or he'll have a roll.

• Horses that get on well will often scratch each other.

Or he will turn to another member of his herd for help with grooming. Known as mutual grooming, two horses will scratch each other using their lips and teeth on sensitive areas such as along the mane or on the back and on the rump.

How hooves stay healthy

Hooves will also look after themselves in the wild. Just like our own fingernails, a horse's hooves are constantly growing, that is why the hooves of horses kept domestically need regular trimming by a farrier.

For wild horses this isn't necessary: they are moving about the whole day looking for food, and due to this constant activity the hooves are automatically worn down.

Caddie's horsey know-how:

In case of danger, run away!!

Did you know that we horses are animals of flight? In the wild, we will only survive if we can run away fast enough from our predators. We still possess this in-built instinct, even if we live in stables or in paddocks.

That's why we take fright so easily at unexpected noises or sudden movements. It's important that you always stay calm around us – and don't tell us off if we shy. We don't mean anything nasty by it, it's just our instincts taking over.

Care of stabled horses

Stabled horses that stand around in their box all day and are only brought out to be ridden, need more looking after than most. These horses miss out on fresh air, sunshine and all of the natural elements that horses living outside are constantly exposed to. That's why it is especially important for stabled horses to be groomed daily. This helps to stimulate their circulation, which contributes to a healthy skin and coat. Besides – grooming is a welcome change to an otherwise routine life!

• Stabled horses should be groomed daily. This not only breaks up their day, but also encourages better circulation for a healthy coat.

• When horses are used to wind and rain, even particularly heavy rain won't bother them.

Horses that are turned out need looking after too!

Horses that are regularly turned out with others have a much better life. They can enjoy the sun on their backs, take the occasional rain shower and share scratching sessions with their friends.

• Horses that are turned out will move about the whole day and look for food.

But even a horse that is living out needs looking after: before riding, his coat should be well groomed, so that saddle and bridle don't rub. If his coat is sweaty after a ride, it needs to be washed down, dried and brushed out again, otherwise his skin will become irritated and start to itch.

Caddie's horsey know-how:

Communicating with horses

We horses may not be able to talk to you, but we understand a lot of what is said to us. From your tone of voice for example we can tell whether we are being given an order, being praised or if we are being told off. An affectionate greeting, a few encouraging words or even the occasional firm "No!" will improve the understanding between you and your horse.

How To

Before grooming

Tie up correctly – remember safety first

Before you start grooming, you need to tie up your horse safely. In many yards there are places set aside for grooming but in others you will just groom outside your stable or with your horse tied up to a fence.

Put a headcollar on your horse with a lead rope attached. The rope should be tied to a solid railing or to a ring that is securely fastened into a wall, but preferably using baler twine or something that will give way if your horse pulls back. To tie up your horse you should use a special knot that will undo quickly in an emergency – for example if your horse gets tangled up in his rope.

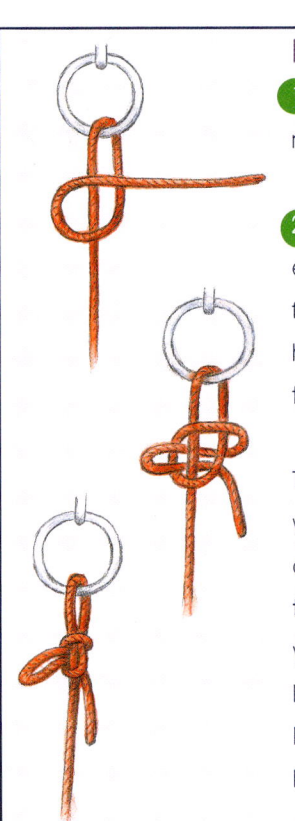

How to tie up your horse

1. First of all, run the rope through the ring and form a loop with the loose end.

2. Now form another loop with the loose end, and slide it from the back to the front through the first loop formed. If the horse tries to move away, the knot will tighten.

The safety knot will undo quickly though when you pull on the loose end. But take care: some horses quickly discover how to undo this knot. To prevent this, when you have finished tieing the knot, pull the loose end through the last loop formed. Most horses won't be able to get the knot undone now

Jacky's tip
Don't panic!

It's perhaps best to use lead ropes with a safety clasp. Horses can't get the clasp undone but you can quickly pull the clasp down to undo.

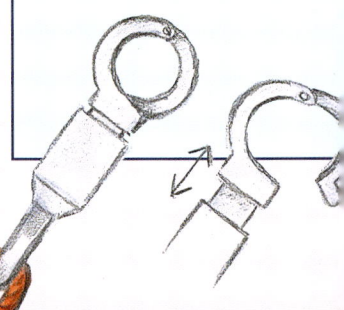

Jacky's tip
Avoid crushed toes

An average horse weighs between 500 and 650 kilos – easily more than 10 times as much as you do! That's why you should always wear sturdy shoes around horses. You never know when a horse may stand on your toes.

Grooming kit

This is what you need to use for grooming:

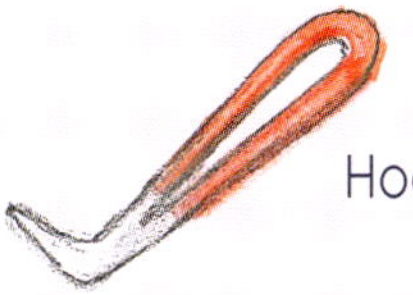

- Hoofpick
- Curry-comb 
- Face brush 
- Water brush 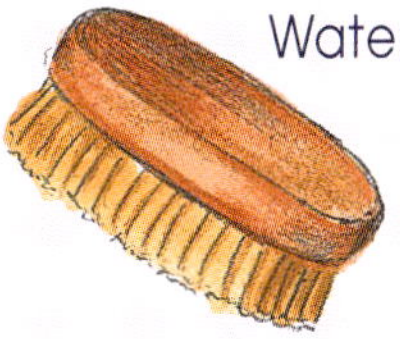
- Dandy brush 
- Two sponges 
- Rubber curry-comb 
- Body brush
- Metal curry-comb
- Grooming mitt 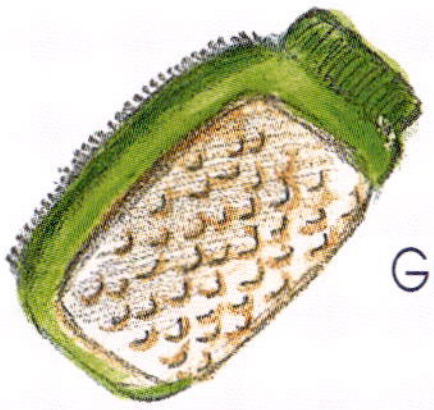
- Sweat scraper

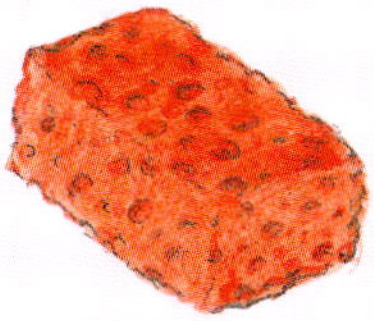

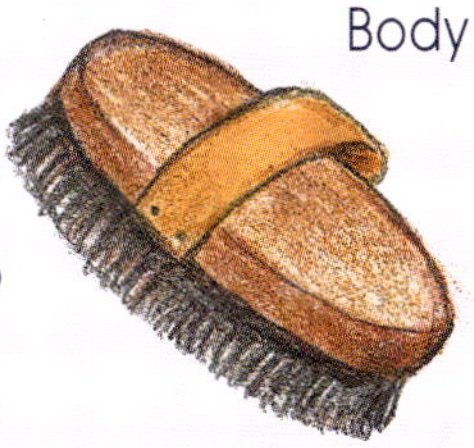

How to look
after your horse

What are the items in your grooming kit called? Write the answers in the empty boxes, one letter to each box. The yellow coloured boxes will reveal the answer to the question: What type of care is most important for your horse?

The solution is on page 30.

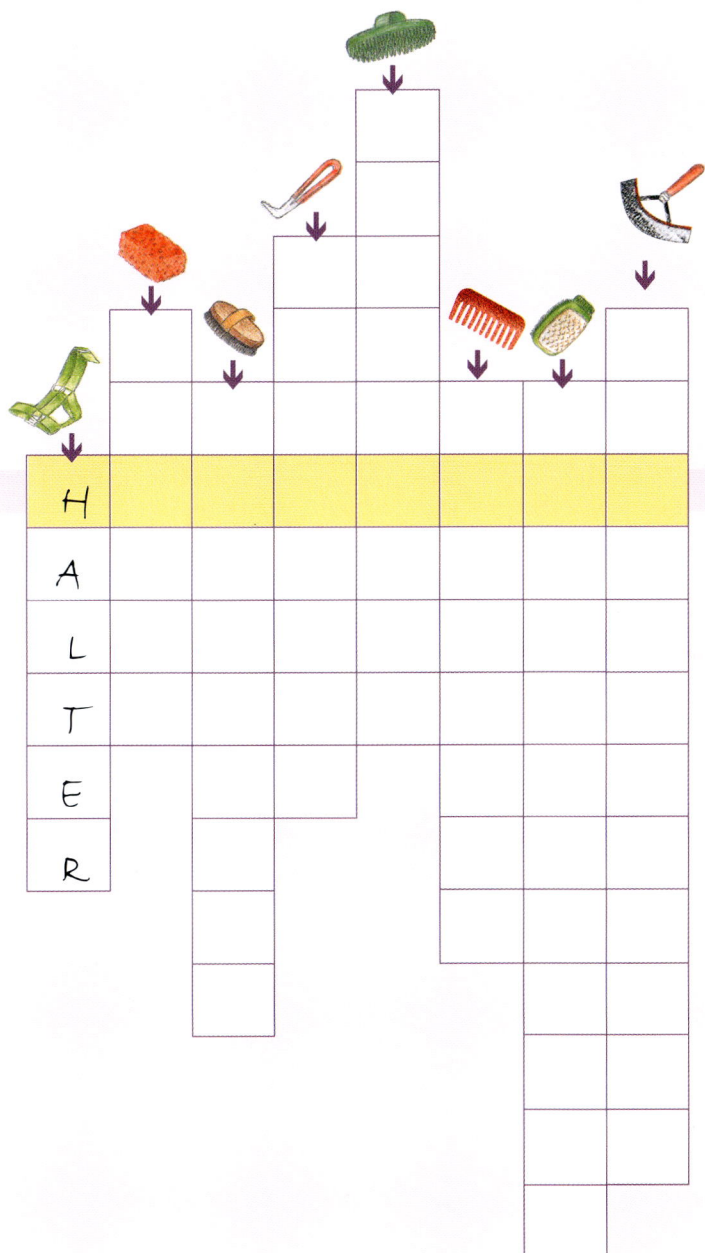

Hoofcare
step by step

Daily hoofcare

Did you know that your horse's hooves need to be checked daily? For horses that are mainly stabled, damp bedding needs to be cleaned out of the hooves so that the hoof doesn't go soft or decay.

And for horses that live outside, they may for example, get small stones stuck in the hooves. Not only can this hurt, but it can lead to infection. So don't forget to pick out your horse's hooves daily!

• When picking out hooves you will stand more securely if you bend your knees slightly.

Lift that leg!

Position yourself next to your horse's front leg so that you are facing his tail. Next, run the hand that is nearest to him down the back of his leg. When your hand nearly reaches his pastern, say "Lift up" or "Hoof" to your horse. He should lift up his leg. (In the picture you can see how you should pick out the right front, or offside, hoof.)

Caddie's horsey know-how:

Picking out hooves – but how?

"He won't let me pick up his feet!" How often have I heard this before? Usually it's followed by a smack on my shoulder or rump, or this two-legged creature tries to pull my leg up using force.

In fact it's more than likely that I am not being awkward, it's just that I haven't understood what I have been asked to do. Each human seems to ask a horse to lift up his leg in a different way: one will touch my leg lightly, while another will fumble somewhere down by my hoof, while a third will even try pulling on my feathers – the hair around my pastern – to get me to lift my leg so they can pick out my hooves. If you find yourself with a horse that doesn't lift up his foot for you when asked, check with someone who knows the horse how they do it. The horse probably just hasn't understood what you are asking for.

Picking out hooves carefully!

Hold the nearside (or left) front hoof firmly with your left hand and pick it out with the hoofpick held in your right hand. In the middle of the sole is the softer part of the hoof sole, known as the frog. It is particularly important to clean the hoof carefully around the frog, as it is a sensitive area. Pick out your horse's hooves in the direction from the frog to the toe.

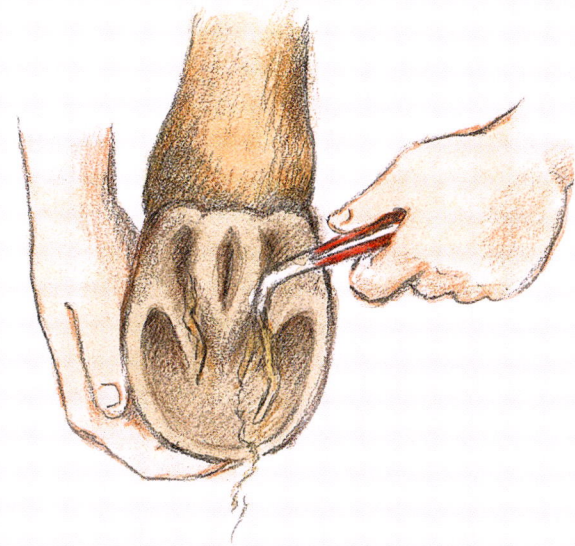

• Clean out stones and dirt from the hoof with a hoof-pick. Be very careful not to damage the sole of the foot.

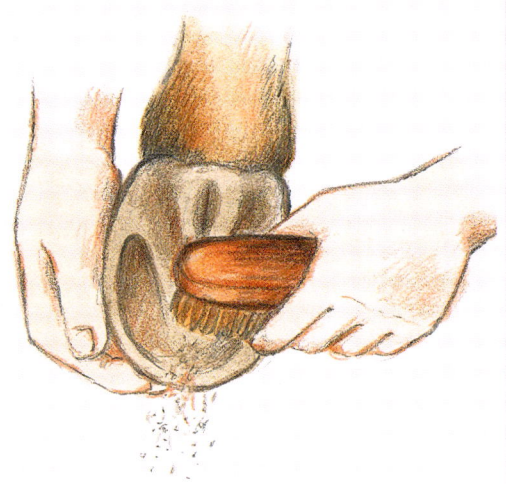

Once you have got the larger lumps of dirt out of the hoof, use a brush to get the hoof totally clean. Always brush away from yourself, otherwise dirt will get in you eyes. Finally place your horse's foot carefully back down on the ground.

After cleaning out the remaining three feet in the same way, grooming his coat is next on the programme.

• Next brush out any remaining dirt from the hoof, especially around and in the middle of the frog.

Jacky's Tip
Hoof oil – yes or no?

In many yards it is still common to oil horse's hooves. Normally, though, the hooves don't need oiling. Oil or grease can clog up the pores of the hoof so that it becomes brittle. Most of the time you can forget about oiling hooves without worrying.

Grooming
step by step
Preparation

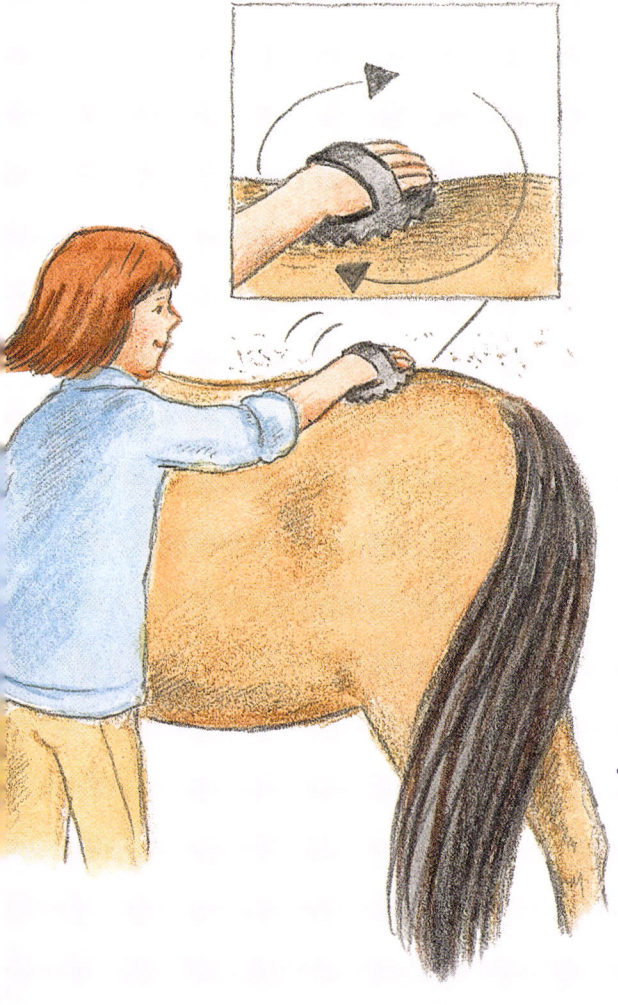

First of all, stand on the nearside of your horse and use a rubber or plastic curry-comb or grooming mitt all over the coat, in a firm circular motion. Begin at the neck and move from the front to the back in the same direction as the hair grows. This gets rid of most of the dirt from the surface of the coat and loosens any dirt from deeper in the coat.

• To loosen up the surface dirt use a curry-comb or grooming mitt. When the coat is particularly dirty or when he is losing his coat, then a curry comb is particularly useful.

Tools for the job

You can use a curry-comb or a grooming mitt for your horse's neck, back, belly and hindquarters. Don't forget to groom under the mane! When you are finished with the nearside, move on to the offside.

Jacky's tip

How to get your horse to move over

So that you can groom your horse all over, he will need to obey your commands to move over. Here's how you ask him : stand next to your horse and tap two fingers against his hindquarters. At the same time, say: "Move over", or "Move round". When the horse responds and steps away, praise him. If he doesn't respond, you will need to be firmer with both your voice and hand. Never just lean against him to try and push him over. He will only respond by leaning back against you, and he is going to be stronger than you...

- Tap your horse on hindquarters to get to move away from

Caddie's horsey know-how

Hey, that tickles!

Watch out: some of my friends are ticklish around their tummies! With horses that you don't know well, you should be especially careful. Before starting to groom, it's best if you ask someone who knows the horse whether it is sensitive or doesn't enjoy being touched in any particular area.

Good legs

Now take a dandy brush and brush your horse's legs. Because they are bonier than the rest of his body, a curry-comb won't get them as clean. Always brush from top to bottom and be sure to stand to the side, especially when doing the rear legs. If your horse is startled by anything and lashes out with his hoof, he is less likely to kick you if you are standing to the side of him.

Don't forget the feathers, and carefully brush the pastern underneath. Horses with a lot of feathering or white leg markings are often particularly sensitive in this area.

• You should never brush legs with a curry-comb — it's uncomfortable for your horse, and it may hurt him.

Caddie's horsey know-how:

Please keep your distance

If there is a sudden movement behind us horses, we may shy or jump. This can mean that we kick out with our hind legs in order to defend ourselves against a suspected predator. That's why you should always keep some distance when grooming and you should never stand directly behind a horse.

Clean through

Now you've got most of the surface dirt off the body and legs you need to get to work with a body brush and curry-comb to get rid of the underlying grime. Hold the body brush in one hand and the curry-comb in the other. Use the body brush in long strokes starting at the neck and work back in the direction the hair is growing – back and down. Every one to two strokes, brush the curry-comb through the body brush to clean out the brush. Bang the curry-comb on a hard surface every now and again to clean it out too. Groom both sides of the horse all over like this, including the legs.

• Use a body brush to clean out the finer dust and dir

Caddie's horsey know-how:

Hard or soft?

When being groomed, every horse has his own preferences. Some horses like to be massaged with strong brush strokes, while others prefer a gentler touch. To discover what your horse likes you need to watch him carefully when grooming. If a horse likes what you're doing, he will stand relaxed with his head lowered. Often his lower lip will droop and he will half close his eyes. If he is not enjoying being groomed then he will probably stand there with his head held high and his muzzle will look tense. In this case you should try to find out how you can make it more pleasant for your horse to be groomed.

Head work

Finally it is the turn of your horse's head. Loosen the head collar so it is hanging around his neck but he is still tied up so he can't run away. Then take a small soft brush and brush carefully around the head, forehead and throat and underneath the head. Be careful though – some horses love having their heads brushed, while others hate it. If you don't know how your horse feels, begin carefully until you know how he will react.

• It's easiest to brush your horse's head when he is tied up like this, using a soft brush.

Caddie's horsey know-how:
Don't overdo it!

Don't overdo grooming on horses kept outdoors in winter. Those horses, who like me are turned out daily, form a natural layer of grease in their coat. This layer protects us from the cold. In the colder months if you clean us up too much you will also clean away this protective layer. That's why you can leave a little grease and dirt in our coat without a guilty conscience and just make sure the surface hair is smooth and clean.

The touch test

When you are finished, run your hand over your horse's body and head. This will let you check that there are no knobbly or lumpy bits of dirt or dried mud left in the coat. This is especially important when you are going to tack up, as any dirt left in the coat could cause rubbing and sores to occur.

- If you run your hands over your horse's coat you will find any spots you may have missed.

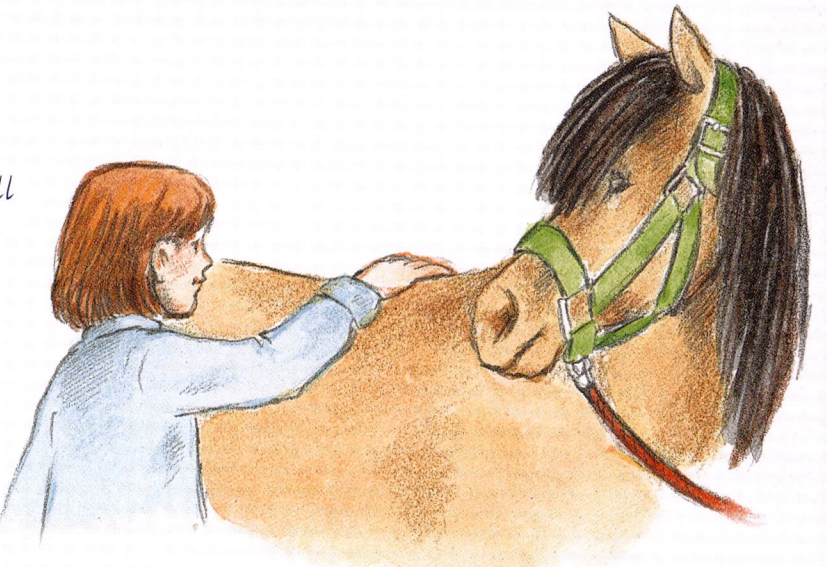

Caddie's horsey know-how:

Why a horse's coat changes

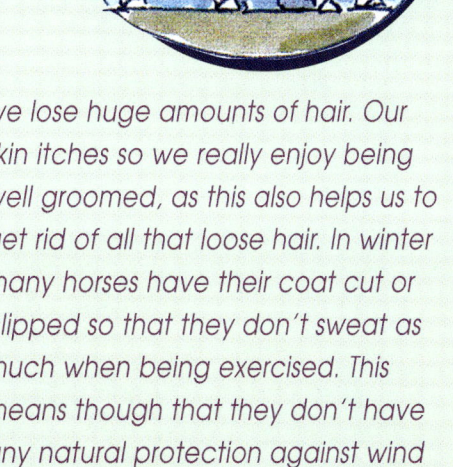

Unlike you humans, horses can't put more clothes on when they get cold. That's why Mother Nature equips us with a thick warm winter coat that grows in autumn before if gets really cold. In spring we shed this coat, because in summer all we need is a fine silky coat. Twice a year then we change our coat, a process also called moulting. In spring especially, this means that we lose huge amounts of hair. Our skin itches so we really enjoy being well groomed, as this also helps us to get rid of all that loose hair. In winter many horses have their coat cut or clipped so that they don't sweat as much when being exercised. This means though that they don't have any natural protection against wind or cold, and must be kept in a stable or rugged up if turned out.

Seasonal change

When you've finished reading this book, enter the answers to the following questions in the circles. When you put the letters from the numbered circles together you'll learn what the other term is for when a horse loses his coat. **You'll find the solution on page 31.**

1. What term refers to a pattern of white hair on a darker background coat?

   7

2. In winter, some horses have their coat cut short. What do you call this?

   4

3. What tool should you use when grooming a mane?

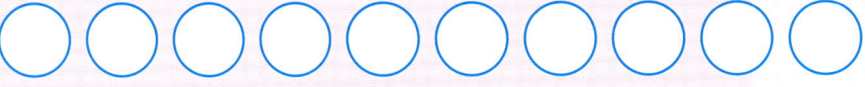

   3

4. When do horses change their fine silky coats for something warmer

○○○○○○
　　　　1

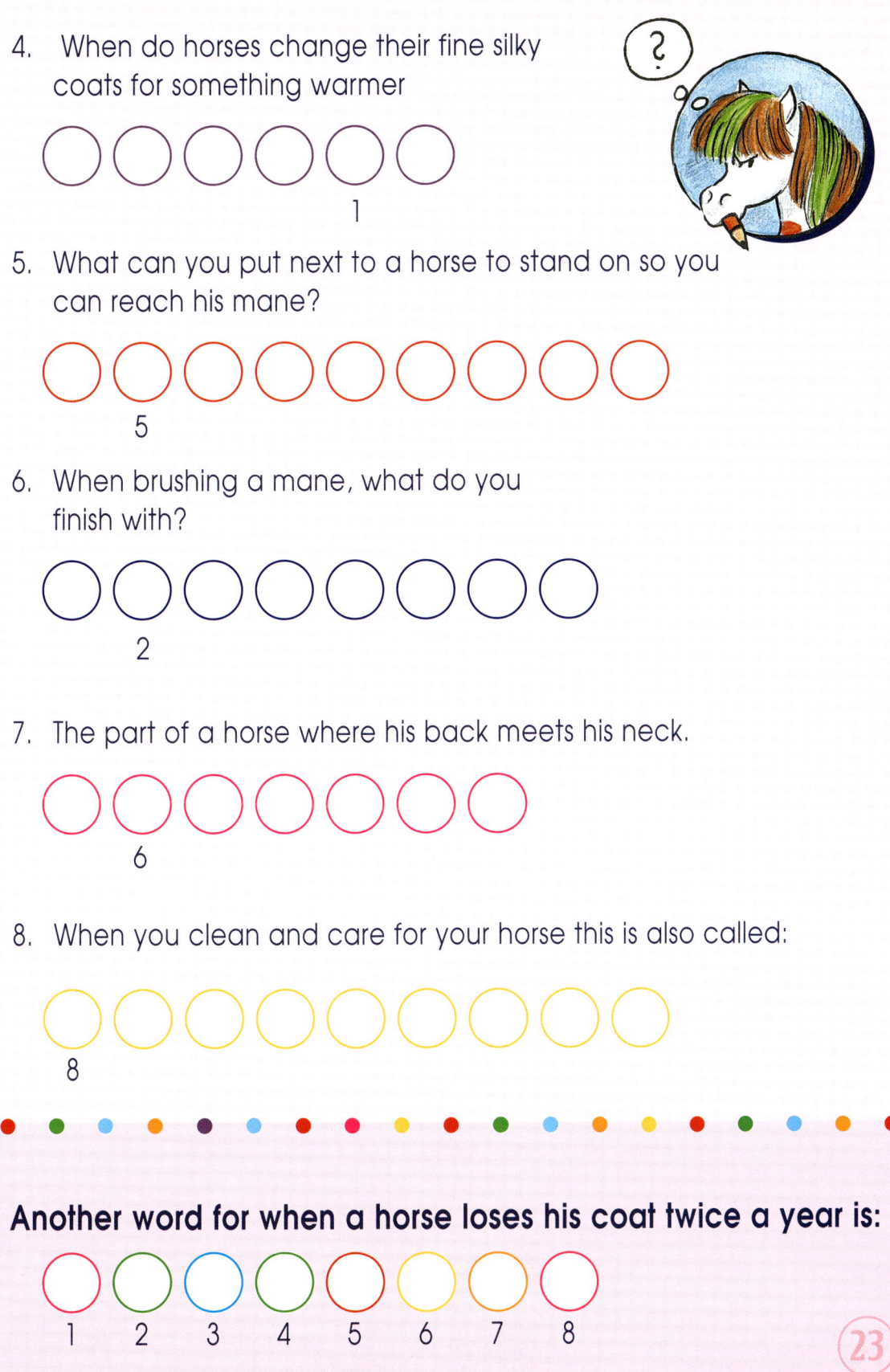

5. What can you put next to a horse to stand on so you can reach his mane?

○○○○○○○○
　　　　5

6. When brushing a mane, what do you finish with?

○○○○○○○○
　　2

7. The part of a horse where his back meets his neck.

○○○○○○○
　　6

8. When you clean and care for your horse this is also called:

○○○○○○○○○
8

Another word for when a horse loses his coat twice a year is:

○○○○○○○○
1　2　3　4　5　6　7　8

Finishing touches

Hair care

Your horse's mane and tail also needs looking after. When brushing out the mane, begin at the withers, in other words where the back joins the neck. Hold a section of mane firmly in your left hand as close as possible to the neck where the hair starts growing. This will stop the mane pulling on the neck and possibly hurting your horse when you start to brush it with your right hand. It's best to use a dandy brush with long bristles for this. Work up the mane towards the head, bit by bit. Tangled hair needs to be untangled carefully by hand as you won't get through it with a brush.

For horses whose mane falls on both sides, you will need to repeat this on the other side. Last of all, brush the forelock out – finished.

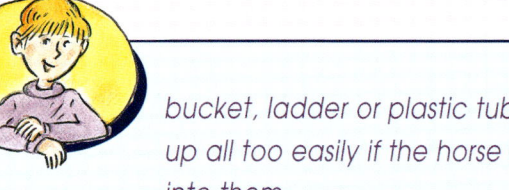

Jacky's tip
How you reach the mane

If your horse is big and won't lower his head for you, you may not find it easy to reach his mane. Don't just climb on the first thing that comes to hand: a bucket, ladder or plastic tub can tip up all too easily if the horse knocks into them.

A bale of straw placed next to your horse is a good idea, or if he is tied up next to a fence, try standing on the lower railing of the fence, providing you have checked that it is strong enough to take your weight.

Tails

With one hand, hold the tail several centimetres above the end. With the other hand comb or brush the bottom bit out and then, moving your hand gradually up the tail, work bit by bit up towards the top, or dock, until all the tail falls free and loose.

Jacky's tip
Finger combing

A mane and tail looks particularly good when, instead of using a brush, you use your fingers to comb it out strand by strand. But here's a warning: for horses with a lot of hair, this can take a long time!

- When brushing the mane or the tail it is important that you hold them above where you are brushing, so you don't hurt your horse accidentally pulling his hair.

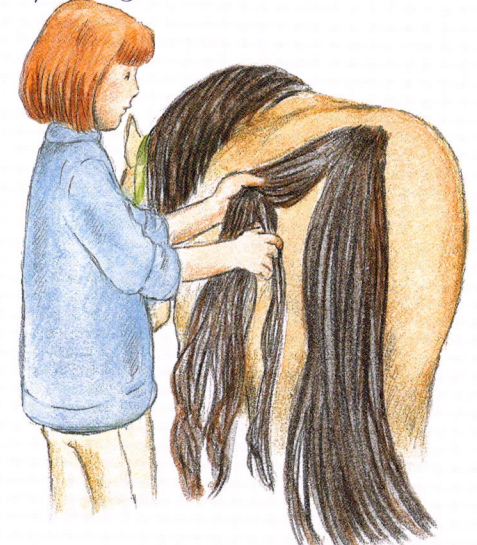

- When you brush out the tail strand by strand with your fingers it looks really nice.

Cleaning eyes and nose

A quick glance at your grooming kit will show you that you have used most of your grooming tools. There are still two sponges to be used, though – so here goes!

One sponge is used for your horse's eyes and nose. Dampen it with water and gently wipe first his eyes and then his nostrils. Be careful that you don't accidentally pull on the fine whiskers and hairs around the eyes, muzzle and nose!

- In cold weather you should wet the sponge with luke warm water.

Care of your horse's rear

You should use the second sponge when the area under and around your horse's tail is dirty. Stand to the side of (never behind) your horse's buttocks, gently lift up the tail and look underneath. If it is dirty, then use the second sponge to wipe it clean.

Caution: never get the two sponges mixed up! It's best if you use two different-coloured sponges, so that you will know which one to use for his face, and which one for his other end.

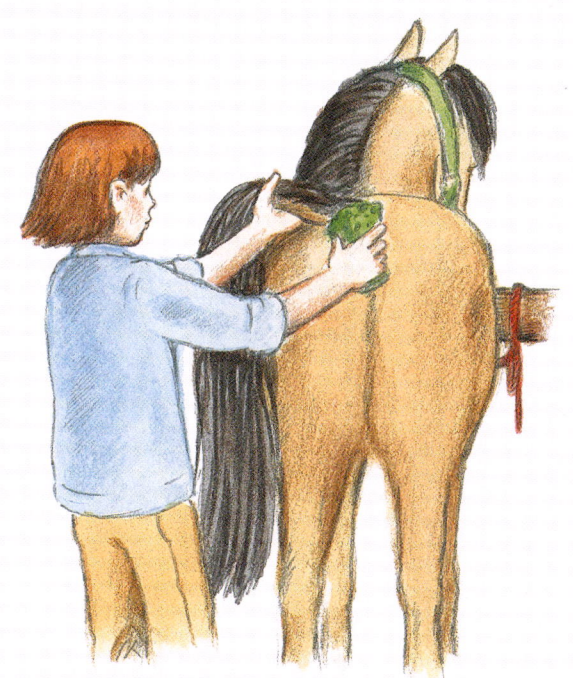

- To clean your horse's bottom you should stand to one side near his hindquarters.

Jacky's tip
One grooming kit per horse

In well-run yards, every horse has his own set of grooming tools, for a good reason. Contagious illnesses or skin ailments, for example ringworm or lice, can be passed on from shared brushes. Even when you have your own grooming kit, if the horse you are riding has his own, use that set for his sake.

Fun & Games

How do horses groom themselves?

Horses can also look after their coat themselves. Answer the questions opposite and when you list the numbered letters in the right order, you will see two ways that horses groom themselves.

You will find the solution on page 31.

Do you know these words?
1. Jacky's favourite pony and the star of this book
2. Long hair on a horse's neck
3. Horse's house
4. Horse's foot
5. What most horses like doing most of the time
6. Pace that comes after walk
7. Striped relative of the horse
8. Baby horse
9. Long-eared relative of the horse
10. Smaller version of a horse
11. Gingery-yellow coloured horse
12. Before gallop comes...

Lösungswörter:

When a horse's skin is itchy, he

1	2	3	4	5

on the ground or he will

6	7	8	9	10	11	12

himself on a tree or against the wall of his stable.

Solutions

Solution from pagees 10/11
What type of care is most important for your horse?

```
              C
              U
          H   R
      S   O   R         S
    P B O Y M G W
  H O O F C A R E
  A N D P O N O A
  L G Y I M E O T
  T E B C B C M S
  E   R K   O I C
  R   U     M N R
      S     B G A
      H       M P
              I E
              T R
              T
```

Solution from pages 22/23

Seasonal Change

The words we were looking for were:
1. Markings
2. Clipping
3. Dandy Brush
4. Autumn
5. Straw bale
6. Forelock
7. Withers
8. Grooming

Another word for when a horse looses his coat twice a year is **moulting**

Solution from pages 28/29

How do horses groom themselves? The words to finish the sentence are **rolls** and **scratch**

Index

A/B
Body brush — 18
Brushing — 14, 15–18

C
Communicating — 7
Curry-comb — 9, 15, 17, 18

D/E
Dandy brunch — 9, 15, 17, 18
Eyes — 26

F/G
Farrier — 5
Feathers — 17
Flight, animal of — 5
Footwear — 9
Grooming kit — 9, 27
Grooming mitt — 9, 15
Grooming, mutual — 4

H
Headcollar — 8
Hoofcare — 5, 12
Hoofcare – natural — 5
Hoof oil — 14
Hoofpick — 9, 12
Hooves – picking up — 12, 13
Hooves – picking out — 13

K/L
Kicking — 17, 18
Knots — 8
Knots – safety — 8
Legs — 17, 18

M/N
Manes – grooming of — 24
Moulting — 21
Moving sideways — 16
Mutual grooming — 4
Nose — 26

P
Pastern — 17

R/S
Riding — 7
Rolling — 4
Shying — 5, 18
Sponges — 9, 26
Stabled horses — 6
Sweating — 7

T
Tails – care of — 25
Ticklish horses — 17
Tieing up — 8
Turned out horses — 6, 7, 20, 21

V/W
Winter coat — 21